Your Clothes Speak

Understanding and Using the Powerful Language of Your Personal Style

Carol Parker Walsh, JD, PhD, FFSF

Also by Dr. Carol Parker Walsh

The Second Act:
Styling YOU From the Inside Out

Copyright © 2016 by Dr. Carol Parker Walsh, All rights reserved. No part of this book may be reproduced in any form without the written permission of the author and its publisher.

This book is dedicated to all you beautiful women out there who deserve to have a wardrobe that represents who you are, achieves your dreams, and makes you look and feel fabulous!

Preface

Clothing is one of our primary human needs. It not only protects us from the elements, it sends very loud messages about who you are, how you feel, what you do, and even what you plan to accomplish for the day. Without even knowing it, our clothes tell stories and make strong visual statements.

We're so used to looking at ourselves (or *not* looking at

ourselves) that we don't realize that others are processing our visual story every day and making conclusions about what they see and who we are that may or may not be true. Whether conscious or unconscious it's most definitely happening.

Does this mean you need to become obsessed about your appearance? Well *obsessed* is a strong word. Since you're in control of how people perceive you before you even open your mouth, it's important to be *mindful* of what you select each morning from your closet. You must be *thoughtful and strategic* about what you decide to wear on a daily basis, particularly if you're an entrepreneur, business leader, or someone looking for a promotion or advancement in their life and/or career. This book was written to help you in that effort. To help you understand the power of your clothes and how to use it to your advantage.

It's time to learn the language of your wardrobe and how to align your authentic self and goals to what you wear. After all, *your clothes speak*. Make sure they're speaking your language.

Table of Contents

1. Introduction

2. What Should Your Clothes Say?

3. The Right Clothing Will Speak to You First

4. Align Your Message and Your Clothes

5. Live in a Negative Free Self-Talk Zone

6. Can We Talk?

Introduction

"Style is primarily a matter of instinct" ~Bill Blass

You know the drill. You wake up, go to your closet, and stare at its contents with a blank and slightly frustrated look. You know what's ahead, you've been there before, and you are not happy. After 45 minutes (the average time it takes women to choose what she's going to wear on any given day), you throw up your hands and grab either the first outfit you pulled out or a variation of what you wore yesterday. You spend the day uncomfortable, uninspired, and unmotivated by your wardrobe choice. Your day didn't go quite as planned and you felt off your game. You're happy to get home so you can take off whatever you were wearing and as you look at that pile of clothes on the floor you sigh because you know you'll have to go back in that closet tomorrow and start the process all over again. Sound familiar?

Sure, you may have received a complement or two on what you were wearing, but internally you weren't feeling great or at your best. You spent the day adjusting, itching, or fidgeting with what you were wearing and overall the energy just felt wrong. I completely understand how you feel because I've been there.

When your clothes represent your authentic essence and style you feel confident, comfortable, and self-assured.

You move about the day with ease and seem to effortlessly accomplish your tasks and goals for the day. Life just feels good.

In my first book, *The Second Act: Styling YOU From the Inside Out* I shared about the importance of finding your authentic style by first examining and embracing who you are. In this book, I'm focusing on the next step, how to use your clothes to accomplish your goals. Understanding the power of your wardrobe, what it communicates, and how to use it strategically in your business and in life is a skill that can and must be learned.

I've helped so many women (and a few gentlemen) find success in their business, walk with more confidence, and fall in love with their wardrobe. It's truly a joy to see them living a life they love and it all started with their clothes.

Clothes are an integral part of life. I had to discover this for myself by applying and using these principles in my own clothing choices and selections. Through trial and error and constant re-examination, I had to find what worked best for me.

Image consultants are trained to focus on your external appearance and what looks best on you. Color, fabric, silhouette, line, and pattern, are all taken into consideration. Outer appearance remains a key consideration but over time I've learned that it's only one piece of the puzzle. It was the combination of my training in Fashion Feng Shui©, my doctoral studies in identity development, sociotechnical systems, as well as, social and analytical psychology, that I began to understand the non-verbal unconscious messages we send out on a day-to-day basis and how they influence how we feel and what we think about ourselves and how we're perceived by others. I'm fortunate to be able to use my skills, training, and experience to provide a holistic and strategic approach to helping people find and use their style to *speak* on their behalf to receive the things they want out of life and business.

Now, if you're a bit skeptical wondering how a colorful scarf, a structured blazer, or well-fitted pair of jeans can help change your business and life just consider how you feel when you put on something that resonates with your personality, preference, and energy. Your clothing has an effect on you because they have energy and in the end we want to surround ourselves with the energy that comforts, moves, matches, and inspires us. Our clothing is connected to us both consciously and unconsciously and speaks to everyone around us, including ourselves. You can feel when what you're wearing is working for you and lifting you up as opposed to putting you down. Just tune in and listen, you'll hear it.

In this book I invite you to understand and listen to the

power of your clothes and how to use them mindfully and thoughtfully in your business and life.

What Should Your Clothes Say?

"Fashion is not something that exists in dresses only. Fashion is in the sky, in the street. Fashion has to do with ideas, the way we live, and in what is happening."
~Coco Chanel

The fashion industry has become rather confusing. Between designers, bloggers, stylists, magazines, and TV series on the subject, it's indeed hard to determine "what not to wear." It's no wonder it takes time and effort to not only discover your *own* personal style language, but how to use that style to communicate who you are and what you want from the world.

When I'm working with a client before we even begin to look at their clothes I first try to learn what makes them tick. I ask a series of questions to get a feel for their personality and preferences. Here's a sample of questions:

- When you first wake in the morning what's the first thing you do?
- How do you greet and spend the day?
- Do you interact with people or work alone?
- Are you the kind of person that loves to multi-task or do you need to focus on one thing through completion?
- Do you want everything to be in order or do you thrive in chaos?

- Do you like routine or do you just go with the flow?

Next, I then turn my attention to current goals, dreams and aspiration, both short and long term. But more on that later.

What does all of this have to do with what you wear? How can you possibly know what to wear if you haven't evaluated your lifestyle or defined your personal and business brand and goals? To ensure your clothes are speaking your language and that you are presenting your best self, you need to pay attention to these aspects of your life.

Don't forget to look around your home and office for additional clues and hints into what represents you authentically. This will provide valuable insight as you begin to assess what's in your closet. Begin to look for any disconnects and places where you see alignment. Are there glimpses of who you are in your closet but an absence of where you want to go? Is your closet reflecting how want to be perceived?

Yes, a lot of questions, but its what's needed to develop the foundation to a wardrobe that is speaking your language. You'll need to start the process again whenever your goals shift or you start a new project or endeavor. This self-reflective work will help you to create a successful wardrobe that's right for you.

Building a wardrobe based on a deeper understanding of who you are, your lifestyle and goals, will ensure your clothes are sending the right message. The process is instinctive and unconscious but authentic and fundamentally you.

The Right Clothing Will Speak to You First

"I think people forget that feeling good is as important as looking good. Although a pretty dress never hurt" ~Stacey Bendet

When we're wearing the right outfit (one that reflects your authentic style), it's like that glorious first bite of a perfectly cooked meal or curling up with your favorite blanket next to a warm cozy fire or slipping into a nice soft fluffy bed. This magical alignment feels good from the inside out. It speaks eloquently to the people around us telling them who we are and what we want without even opening our mouth. As soon as we put on the right thing we know it. It happens in an instant and it's amazing. It's like butter, or as Mike Meyer's Saturday Night Live character Linda Kaufman on *Coffee Talk* would say, "it's like buttah."

After the self-discovery process, I next work with my clients to tune into how they *feel* in their clothes. Whether shopping or working in a closet it's important to examine how you *feel* before you determine how it looks. It's imperative to put on your clothes, avoid the mirror, and tune into how the fabric, cut, and style feels. We're not trained to consider our feelings around what we wear, just what it looks like. However, the feelings are there if we'd just take the time experience them. Too often we ignore our feelings and instead allow what we see in the mirror, or worse the opinion of others, to cloud our thinking and minimize what we know in heart to be true.

We're often influenced to purchase things we've seen on celebrities in magazines, fashion bloggers, or a colleague whose style we admire. We love the look and believing it will look just as good on us, we decide to try it out for ourselves. It's an amazing sweater, jacket, or skirt but when we put it on we immediately get the sense that it's not quite right. This is one of the key reasons we only wear about 20% of what's in our closet.

Many people struggle with a closet filled with nothing to wear. Still searing to find those pieces that are just right. Take a look in your closet and ask yourself:

- Do I have a closet filled with things my girlfriend said I looked great in?

- Items, convinced by the sales associate, that I looked amazing in?
- Undesirable gifts bought for me by my loved ones, family, or friends?
- Am I holding on to things for sentimental or irrational reasons but will never wear and probably never will?

The energy of our clothes speaks to our soul so it's critical to rid ourselves of those items that don't feel right, are misaligned with our soul, and are not sending positive, uplifting, and life-giving energy our way.

Julie (a fictional name) had a closet filled with other's ideas of what would look great on her. She never defined her own style and because of her small shapely frame she was often told *anything* would look great on her. She shopped and made purchases on the advice of others and was consistently complimented on what she wore but she confided in me that she literally hated everything in her closet and dreaded getting dressed in the morning. After our first session together Julie discovered her true style and which colors, fabrics, and silhouettes felt and looked fabulous on her. In tears she thanked me because for the first time in her life she understood why she hated her clothes. For years she thought it her shape or her look. She internalized the idea that nothing worked because of her, instead of understanding it was because her clothes were not speaking her language or speaking to her soul.

Now having said this, I don't want to dissuade you of the fact that what you wear has to look great on you. As I mentioned with Julies we found what looked amazing on her. As an image consultant I'm trained to ensure you look amazing. It's one of the pieces of the puzzle that I work with my clients to solve. However, what I want to make clear is that what it looks like is not the *only* thing that matters. In fact, what looks good is not even the *first* thing that matters. It's about the feeling you get when you're wearing the item; and that feeling doesn't come from suggestions, persuasion, or insistence. When we try to wear things that are not in alignment with who we are, don't speak to our heart or feel right to our soul, then it's simply not right to wear. Your clothes should speak to *you* first.

So do this, take a scan of your closet. Try on all of your clothes and initially skip the mirror. Don't cheat yourself out of this important step. Ask yourself first and foremost, "How does it feel?" If it doesn't feel right, don't keep it. Plain and simple.

Once you've gone through everything and found those pieces that feel like "buttah", the next stage is to align our clothes with your objectives and goals.

Align Your Message and Your Clothes

"Fashion is what you're offered four times a year. Style is what you choose. It's what you make of it once you've learned what to accept and ignore." ~Lauren Hutton

Yes, it's absolutely important to have alignment with the clothes you wear. Alignment is that symbiotic relationship between self, clothes, and goals. In other words, who you are, how you present yourself to the world (your personal and professional brand), and the attainment of your aspirations. When you achieve this alignment your clothes will start working for you. You'll begin to position yourself for the achievement of your vision, goals, and dreams.

While in the process of working through your closet it's imperative to keep your business and life goals at the forefront of your mind. The things that you want to see happen and accomplish in the future. In fact, repeating your *style mantra* (i.e., I initiate change or I attract clients daily) out loud as you choose your outfit for the day will help you toward that end.

Taking this strategic approach to your wardrobe will ensure you're prepared for the opportunities and encounters that will come your way. Write down where you want be and what you want to accomplish:

- Today
- Next week
- Next month
- Next six months
- For the year

Then consider which pieces in your closet will serve you effectively in achieving these things.

Can you begin to see how your clothes can aid in getting the results you want in your life or achieve the success you want in your business?

Take Barbara (not her real name) for example; a

successful realtor who, for lack of a better phrase, lost her style mojo. After working together and building this alignment with her authentic self, her clothes, her brand, and her goals she remarked that she had her best selling season achieving a seven-figure year. Her goals were to increase sells, fall back in love real estate, and feel confident selling million dollar homes. That's exactly what we focused on when we rebuilt her wardrobe and ensured it was in alignment with her goals.

What you wear will speak to you and influence others thoughts and impressions of you. If you're not making these conscious choices you run the risk of sending the wrong message and being viewed incorrectly. You'll unintentionally thwart the positive energy and outcomes that you've been working so hard to attain.

Once discovered, your authentic style will remain constant. This will make it easy for you to shop and maintain a consistent and very wearable wardrobe. You'll be comfortable and confident in what you wear. What will change, however, are your goals and intentions; your aspirations and the things that you are working on week-by-week, month-by-month and year-by-year. As you redirect or readjust things in your life it will be important to make the necessary tweaks in your wardrobe to safeguard the connection and conversation between self, clothes, and goals.

Live in the Negative Free Self-Talk Zone

"Only wear clothes that make you feel alive." ~Valentino Garavani

If you're not feeling fabulous in what you're wearing it will transcend into every aspect of your life. Instead, however, of identifying the issue as a clothing misalignment, we tend to turn that negative energy against ourselves. Have you heard yourself say, "I don't look good in anything? I can never find anything that fits me. I hate the way I look." I know most of us, including me, have or continue to struggle with some degree of a negative self-image. The truth of the matter is you're beautiful (stop for a moment and say it to yourself). It's sad to me that most women fail to see their innate glory, beauty, and significance. But the fault is not our own; it's the countless images we encounter that tell us something's not quite right. Finding clothes that speak to us should not be a process of guilt and shaming but of joyful exploration and evolution.

I often hear women say, "When I lose some weight I'll work on my closet." Another comment I commonly hear is, "If I had $5000 of course I'd look amazing." The truth is neither of these statements are relevant or have any impact on looking fabulous. Looking fabulous is merely a reflection of feeling fabulous on the inside. It's the external reflection of someone who has internally embraced her beauty and significance. It's not about being fashion obsessed, losing or gaining weight or having a million dollars; it's about finding your passion for YOU. Our clothing must speak to the person we are *right now* and are currently working to become. Life's too short not to.

Rather than negative self-talk like I hate shopping, I can't find anything to wear, or I need to change some aspect of my body, you be able to enjoy shopping because you'll know exactly what is right for you and your body. You'll no longer have to waste time trying on thousands of items that are not in alignment with who you are or what you're trying to achieve. You'll feel empowered to go into a store or through your closet owning those pieces that represent who you are now while releasing what no longer works or suits the authentic you. While in dialogue with your clothes you'll no longer have to subject yourself to negative self-talk, guilt or shame. You'll joyfully release what doesn't work and embrace what feels right and speaks life to you.

Now for those of you wondering about those well-meaning gifts you received from your husband or loved one, I give you permission to release those too. I know it can be hard to part with something that your spouse gave you (and expects you to wear), as well as that sweater or scarf you're mother gave you while she was still alive. I've personally experienced both scenarios. Keep this thought in mind: We are doing the best that we can for the people that we love if we first love and honor ourselves. Ultimately our loved ones will support our wearing things that genuinely reflect and embrace who we are because they want us to be happy. Share how much you appreciate the thought and the items they so lovingly gave to you. Help them understand your authentic style. Express your desire for a deep meaningful relationship that has space for you without having to compromising who you are by wearing something that doesn't genuinely reflect your newfound style. Everyone will be better off for your honesty, and you'll no longer be forced to wear something that never really worked for you.

Whenever you start to feel weak on this point just

remember. It is not about your wonderfully well-intentioned gift-giver, it's about giving yourself permission to present your best self to the world. Those who love and support you will honor your efforts to always bring your best self in everything you do.

Can We Talk?

"The way we dress affects the way we think, feel, and act; and the way others respond to us."
~Judith Rasband

There are a few final thoughts I'd like to leave with you. First, become a detective and discover who you are in relation to your wardrobe. Before you open your mouth, your clothes will speak for you. Be sure it's the story you want to share. We all want to feel confident, powerful, and loved and frankly we all deserve it. It starts first, however, with you and your clothing choices. Take the time, the energy and the investment to make sure that you are surrounding yourself with things that reflects who you are, what you want, and where you are going in life and business. Your clothes speak and you want to make sure their words are embracing you with love, inspiring you to action, and supporting your success.

Second, don't be afraid to look and feel fabulous. Power comes from putting yourself first. I know this can be challenging for women and particularly those who think it's vain, silly, or selfish to invest time and energy to their clothing and wardrobe choices. In her book, *Return to Love*, Marianne Williamson wrote some of the most powerful words I've every read. When you think of your own self-worth and whether there's something to be gained in investing in yourself, loving you, strategically creating a functional wardrobe, and believing in your own beauty, take a moment to consider her words.

"Our deepest fear is not that we are inadequate. Our deepest fear is that we are powerful beyond measure. It's our light, not our darkness that most frightens us. We ask ourselves, 'Who am I to be brilliant, gorgeous, talented, fabulous?' Actually, who are you not to be? You are a child of God. Your playing small does not serve the world.

There is nothing enlightened about shrinking so that other people won't feel insecure around you. We are all meant to shine, as children do. We were born to make manifest the glory of God that is within us. It's not just in some of us; it's in everyone. And as we let our own light shine, we unconsciously give other people permission to do the same. As we are liberated from our own fear, our presence automatically liberates others."

Finally, stop struggling with your value, with your greatness, and with your purpose. Let's work to end your frustration with a closet full of things that you don't wear, that fail to represent you and what you want to achieve, and fail to present you in ways you know you want and should be seen. Use your clothes to realize your goals, dreams, and intentions and create a business and life you love. Know who you are, whose you are, and know your purpose. Reflect on what you want in business and in life. Feel the clothes as you wear them, listen to what they say, and walk with confidence in your style. Let your clothes speak and be prepared for who's listening.

-END-

Made in the USA
Las Vegas, NV
05 November 2021